Diamond's Everlasting Foot Prints

Shelia Hampton

Diamond's Everlasting Foot Prints

Createspace

www.createspace.com

Diamond's Everlasting Foot Prints

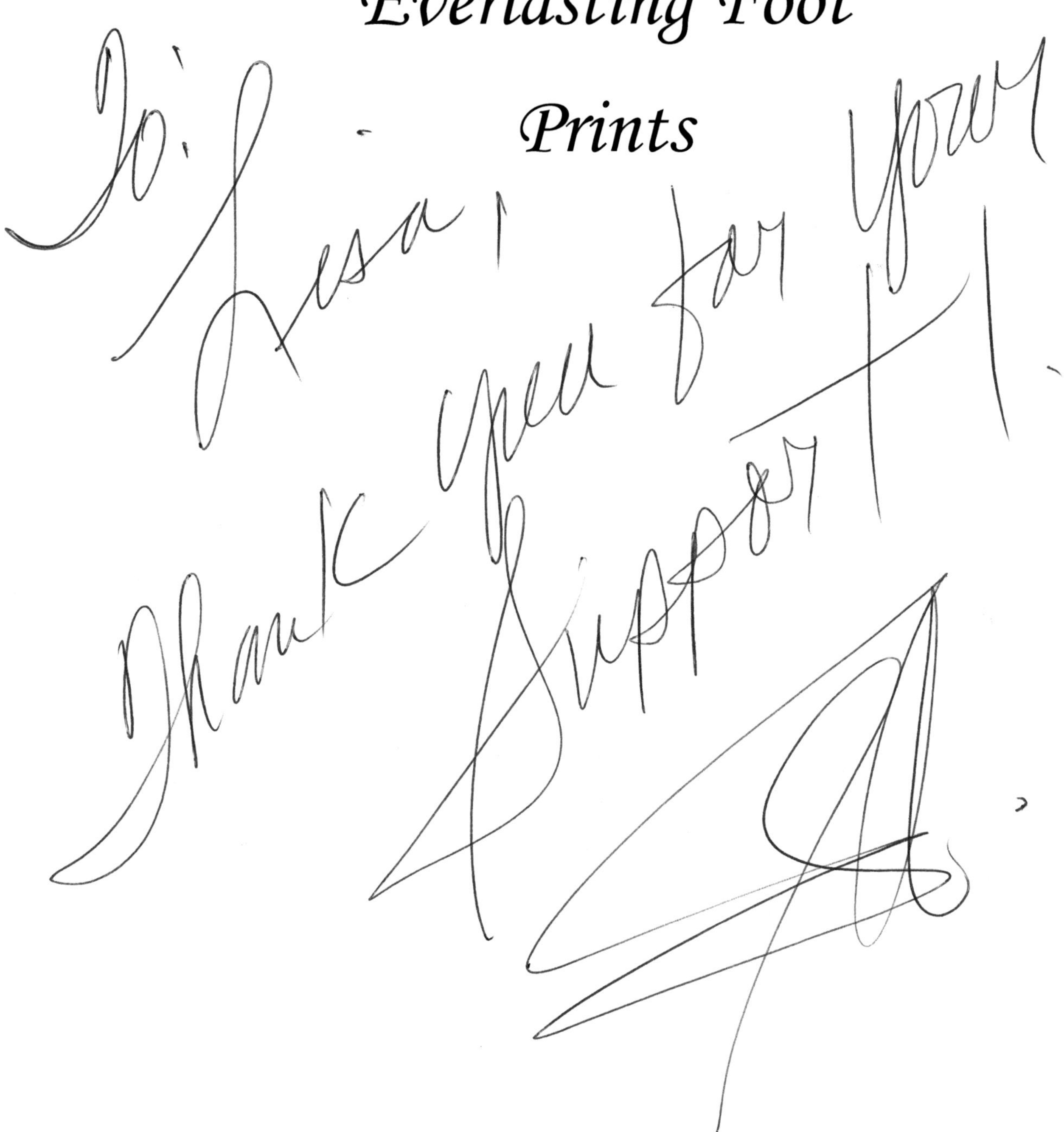

Shelia Hampton

Diamond

Shelia Hampton

Diamond's Everlasting Foot Prints

Unless otherwise noted, scripture quotations are

taken from the King James Version of the Bible

ISBN - 13: 978-1523697939

ISBN - 10: 1523697938

To purchase additional books:

www.createspace.com

or

hamp.shelia@gmail.com

301-848-5016

Editors

Barbara J. King

Shelita Chandler

Cover Design: Shelia Hampton

Photographs by Shelia Hampton

Published By:

Createspace Publishers

Dedication

This book is dedicated to several special people, my wonderful husband Grant Hampton, my precious children Duane Hampton and Shelita Chandler, my granddaughter Danielle Chandler, my mom Lois Sinclair, and to all the pet and animal lovers worldwide.

Acknowledgements

First, I want to thank my Lord and Savior who showers me with unconditional love in all aspects of my life. I thank Him for the vision to write this book about my beloved Diamond. D.D., "You are the inspiration who has led me to write this book."

Certainly, I thank my loving husband and friend Grant L. Hampton, my two beautiful children, Duane Hampton and Shelita Chandler, for inspiring and encouraging me to write this book. It is you, my loving family, who motivate me to do positive things daily. I thank you all for your life commitments that make my life worth living.

Many special thanks go to Audrey Mayo and Karen Entwisle for placing Diamond in my life. If not for them, I would not have had this opportunity to write about "these everlasting footprints" which has given me so much joy.

Lastly, I thank Alcide de Jean King Jr. and his wife Barbara J. King of King Illustrations in Memphis, TN for their invaluable professional services with this publication.

Introduction

On Sunday April 19, 2015, I had awakened at 7:58 am to the warmth of the sun shining through my window, to a cool morning breeze, and to the wondrous sounds of birds chirping. Aha! Right at that very moment, I knew for sure that in each new day, there is always "new life" in each breath that we take and that it doesn't stop, here, on this earth.

This book is written out of my love for a special pet that I recently lost to death. We had a special bond of love that is too complex and not so easy to put into words. Therefore, I have chosen to use photos that will help you visualize just some of what we shared. It is my hope that healing will take place within me as I write each word in this book for you to comprehend. You see, I was very grief-stricken when I lost my special friend and little girl, appropriately, named Diamond; she was a true, precious gem. In addition, this book is for those who value the unconditional love of family and close friends.

As you journey with me, it is my hope that something from this book will bring healing and joy to your life. It is my belief that healing is from God. I believe that He sent Diamond into my life for that purpose- healing: for and from things that were known and unknown to me. Sincerely, it is my prayer that by, "the showing and telling," of Diamond's life and times, her story will encourage healthy healing for anyone who desires it.

Diamonds are treasured, rare gems that can be useful, powerful tools. They should be held close to your heart. God truly loves us and holds us close to His heart. Sometimes, the Lord will give us a "diamond in the rough." Sometimes, that diamond is you - you were in the rough! I believe that everyone has a diamond that he or she cherishes very much. Some diamonds shine very brightly and make life easy for us. Others need polishing and rubbing to make their brilliance show their true potential. My Diamond's everlasting footprints provided so much joy because she gave unconditional love and service to all she came in contact. Diamond, I thank you for illuminating this world and my world during your brief stay with us.

We all have to go through trials because afterwards, God will have strengthened us to face obstacles so we can help others. I believe that life experiences help you to assist others as you learn from them yourself.

Finally, one of my goals is to convey to you, that my Diamond has left an "Everlasting Foot Print" upon my heart and others who she has touched along her little way. Hopefully, this imprint will empower and encourage animal lovers who have lost a pet because of death, to accept the loss and to celebrate its life in the best possible way.

Through my own grieving experiences, I have found some helpful strategies that I pray will contribute to your success as you endure and learn during your grief period until you get to that peaceful and joyous place on your healthy- healing journey while letting go of what you had no control over in the first place. Sincerely, it is my prayer that by sharing Diamond's life and times and the wonderful relationship that we shared, it will encourage and contribute to your success as you endure your grief-journey to your healthy, healing-journey.

Table of Contents

Promising Possibilities

Diamond came to the workplace with hopes to become a service dog to render therapeutic services to the students. It was a surprise discovery to find out that she did not really work with children. Since she was unable to perform her duties as a service dog, therefore, she was offered to me.

Her owners needed to place her in a home but were a little reluctant because she was very snappy towards everyone. In my heart, I wanted to take her home, but I was a little hesitant at first. So then, I said to a very special co-worker, "I want this dog and would like to take her home for the weekend to see how it will work out." As I picked the dog up, she cried. I gave her much love. It was then that I decided to make this 18 months old Pomeranian a special part of my family.

Once I took her home, she opened up a completely new, beautiful world for me. She amazed me every day with her amusing ways. At this point, Diamond was able to perform her duties in the capacity as a service dog. Service dogs help individuals with limitations or disabilities like blindness, hearing difficulties, seizures, epilepsy, and other physical or mental disorders.

From the time I decided to take her home and with each passing day, she had a very special print in my heart. This little girl visited many places with me such as: work, church, hospitals, shopping, restaurants, and she went to several events. She was always helpful wherever she went. She has even attended a community event and got some press time while there! LOL (Laugh Out Loud)! Each picture placed in this book has an everlasting print upon my spirit. I want you to see how many of them that you can identify with in hopes that each, or some may impact your life in a helpful manner.

Life's Specials Touch

Every lasting footprint has a special touch. Have you ever wondered why animals are placed here on earth? I believe that each print has a special story. Well, this is Diamond's story. Animals do speak, feel, touch, and have deep feelings.

Care for one Another

These two are very special friends who really care for one another. This little one always puts Diamond first, and they see things eye to eye. How adorable they are while always showering each other with great affection and love! If you look at this picture closely, you can see the bond that Danielle and Diamond have as they speak to each other in their own love-language.

Who Touched Me--"Diamond"

Diamond has touched my heart in a very special way. Each day a different print was deposited in my life. The love she shared was always absolute, unconditional, and never limited. This little girl gave me unconditional love with much affection.

Walking On A Cloud

Diamond knew how to walk, as if she was walking on a cloud. When she decided she wanted a treat, Diamond would walk, stand, dance, smile, and give a show. Just say "TREAT," and you would have to give a treat and she would give you a really good treat! Diamond only liked liver treats, and all of her food had to be on the same line or brand of food, or she would not eat it. It had to be made of chicken! What a finicky girl! Yes, and she was very spoiled!

Something for Everybody

At Christmastime Diamond got a wonderful gift. She received a red sweater that matched her best friend's coat. They went to the park for their "Play Date." They climbed up and slid down the slide. They were amazed and excited about all the new things in the park. It was a little brisk outside, and they enjoyed rustling the leaves as they blew. As they played, Danielle would often ask Diamond, "How do you like playing at the park, today?" Then, Diamond would give her a big lick on the face to show how much she liked it! They shared lots of love!

Blessing

It was such a blessing to have Diamond's love, protection, and service. She loved being outdoors during the holiday seasons. I think that Christmas was her favorite one. If only she could tell me what she sees that had captivated her so much!

Cherish the Moment

Diamond, while on vacation at Myrtle Beach, South Carolina, would get up early each morning and cherish the moments on the beach. She would walk along the shore, watch the sunrise, smell the crisp air, and look at the wonderful waves. I believe that in her mind, she would value these instances by taking full advantage of all the rewards that this "getaway" provided.

Best Friends

Friends communicating and sharing the sunset! Watching and telling each other sunny secrets. I thought I heard her say, "Did you hear me Diamond?" If you look closely, you can see Diamond's ears were perked-up as she listened to Danielle, then she became cheerful.

A Mother's Touch

A mother has a touch like no other. When I touched Diamond and put my loving arms around her, I could see the sparkle in her eyes letting me know that all was well with her; always having that feeling of security, comfort, and love.

Pack of Friends

Diamond had her own little pack of Pomeranian friends that she would take afternoon walks with through our community. These extraordinary friends would meet for walks and talks. Of course, they had their own language that only they completely understood. It was amazing to listen to them communicate with each other as they played and followed each other around. If Diamond didn't go to their houses, her friends would come to hers. They seem to say to each other, "Come in, look around, and let's go check things out!" As I observed the joy in their little lives, I could see that life sure has its beauty about it, you just have to look for it! The Bible tells us in Psalm 28:7:

" The Lord is my strength and my shield; my heart trusted in him, and I am helped: therefore my heart greatly rejoiceth; and with my song will I praise him (KJV)." Therefore, to praise God--just live your best life; enjoy it and do good-- to yourself and others.

Beauty of Life

Reflection: A student did a special report about Diamond at one of our local private schools. After the report, her classmates were amazed to find out how helpful this service dog performed her duties. They did not know that service dogs carried out so many beneficial services.

Great Journey

We always enjoyed the seaside and the prints in the sand! Just look at these prints! Even the sand can't cover them up! There are tons of prints out there on the beach. As we sat and enjoyed the cool breezy waves in Myrtle Beach, South Carolina, my husband, Diamond, and I tried to figure out the significance of each print left in the sand. What did they mean? Why had those people come to the beach? What was the sand and the ocean telling us? It was telling us to relax and enjoy the serenity by the sea, and have another great vacation at the beach!

The Sun Will Shine

Where is Diamond? You can't hide Diamond. The sun will shine, and I will find you! Diamond tried to hide under her costume. I said to her, "I see you!" She smiled and put her little nose out for air as if to ask, "Is it time for us to be off for a walk now, mom?"

Understanding Life

Diamond seemed to be unable to understand her duty, which was to help us watch the three day old, newborn baby. When the baby cried, Diamond looked mystified and helpless. She waited patiently until we were finally able to satisfy the infant. What a wonderful bond from the very beginning with those two! That was a new and exciting experience for her.

Thankful

Diamond seemed to be very thankful for everything, every job, and every journey. Diamond, "You did a great job, and I thank you for all of your help." You made life so very special for your family and others. I thought that I had rescued you when you needed a home and did not want to be bothered all the time. Let the truth be told--- you rescued me with your unconditional love and warmth.

Miracle

The park was a great place to be in the evenings for Diamond and her friends. They enjoyed going to the park just like children. Diamond always seemed to enjoy being the leader of her pack. She would gladly be the first to go down the slide and wag her tail in enjoyment afterwards. Then she would walk back up the stairs, and wait her turn for another go! Once her friends went down the slide, she would be elated to have another turn.

Each Day

Each new day was a great day after a good haircut, a good meal, and a good walk. Diamond loved getting treats. She would patiently wait for a snack, and then look at me as if to say, "What's next?" When one of my family members was very ill, Diamond helped to save his life. She had sensed his sickness so, she jumped on the bed where he was and kept licking him to keep him awake and alert. She stayed right by his side for several hours until help arrived. Because of Diamond's vigilance, he received timely medical attention that saved his life.

God used Diamond for two more life-saving miracles for us. Something was burning on the stove, and she made us aware of that hazard. Secondly, she alerted us when an earthquake was erupting in our area. Diamond was truly a God-sent who loved and took care of her family and friends.

One Day at a Time

Diamond was just resting and relaxing in Williamsburg, Virginia as she looked off the balcony platform, watched the golfers on the golf course, and seemed to say to herself, "What a great life to be smacking small balls!" Then, Diamond was thinking, "Hey, what was that sound? Oh, it was just my stomach rumbling; it's almost time to eat!" Mom!

Imagine

While trying to put on this great outfit, Diamond was thinking, I wonder which way it goes? Well, I imagine it is this way. I think this is the top with the white fur around the neck. Yes, I think that's right! I really like this furry, red, white, and silver lacy dress for the Christmas holidays. Thanks Mom!

Lifetime

Diamond was a lifetime sports fan. This is her resting after attending a game. She was tired after a very long night. She was a #1 fan of the W.W. basketball team in Washington DC. She really had enjoyed sitting in the 100th section at the V. Center. Also, I have to mention how much she enjoyed the boxing matches at various events in New Jersey.

Relationships

"It was always great to have good relationships with people. As I explored my community, I was well known. I used to like the attention that my red outfit attracted for me. Red was my favorite color to wear around town because it stood out. I was particularly well-liked no matter where I went!"

Impressions

Prints can make you strong. There are prints everywhere and in everything that you do. Have you ever watched snowflakes flutter in the air? They have their own unique prints. Have you ever watched raindrops come streaming down? Check out the prints that it leaves behind. When it is cold outside, prints can be found in the ice or mud on the ground. Look at the imprints in the sand as you take a stick and make a man. Observe the carpet in your house after you step on it. You won't believe the faces or objects that it projects, even the floor after it's wet. If you look closely, you'll notice, after you walk on it, that you may see a person, animal, or some print that is left behind. When you see a print, each one tells a story. Just look at it very closely and ask yourself, "What does this print mean"? I am sure that print will leave a lasting impression or thought on you.

As people, we make noble impressions on things from the very beginning of our lives. I believe God placed Diamond here on earth to leave great impressions on people that she came in contact along her journey. Well done, my Diamond, well done!

Life

Life has been great! Thanks Mom and all whose lives God has enabled me to touch during my trip through this wonderful life.

My Healing Journey

Four Simple Steps that Help

Grief over the loss of a pet is REAL! I never knew that I would be facing something like this. The intense heartache is so personal, and stronger than one could possibly imagine. It truly feels like you are losing a close family member or relative. For people who do not understand the animal-lover's grief, this book will bring to light our genuine pain. Moreover, it will provide four simple steps that I am taking along my healing journey.

As a mentor, I want to share my faith with you. Faith is a conviction of confidence in a higher power above you. For me it is a strong trust and reliance on my God of the Heavens. My biblical teachings about faith says that, "Now faith is the substance of things hoped for, the evidence of things not seen (Hebrews 11:1 KJV.)" Friends, believe me, my sorrow is not over. I know that with the help of God that I will make it through, somehow!

Now, I want to share four steps from my journey that are helping me through my grief-recuperation that I hope will help you:

1.) Live in the reality of the moment. Laugh, cry, or break something! Shout! Do whatever it takes to get the sadness and hurt out of your system. Allow yourself to, "totally," confront your loss. I lost my beloved Diamond, who happened to be my beloved pet dog and friend. It does not matter if you lost a close relative, pet, friend, or some object that you loved, you can get over it. I hope that this scripture, "I can do all things through Christ which strengtheneth me (Philippians 4:13, KJV)," will help you get through this phase. You must meditate on, and believe these powerful words, do not just say them.

2.) Develop a support system. You do not have to go through this grief-journey on your own. Talk to loved ones, friends, church members, anyone who you feel will be sympathetic to your concerns. Soon, you will become strong and that which seemed impossible to get over becomes bearable. Eventually, you will get over your loss. Try to remember the good times that you and your loved one had together. You will be able to move-on, and enjoy the beautiful life that God has given you. Remember this awesome promise from the Lord, "But my God shall supply all your need according to His riches in glory by Christ Jesus (Phillipians 4:19)."

3.) Take the time to feel, relax, and reflect on your hurt. Know that grief is a part of life. Understand that what you are feeling, or going through when you lose something or someone that is dear to you, is a fact. Grief is a feeling of unhappiness, and sometimes it can make you become isolated from those you love because you think that those close to you don't care, or truly understand what you are experiencing. Nevertheless, take time to work out your sorrow and pain. Keep this scripture in mind, "And the peace of God, which passeth all understanding, shall keep your hearts and minds through Christ Jesus (Philippians 4:7)."

4.) Make an adjustment to preserve the positive part of your relationship with the loss of your loved one or thing. Find that creative space within you. Create something in loving memory of him, her, or it. I chose to write this book with fond memories, spiritual messages, and practical poetry as a way to show my continuing love, affection, and connection to my Diamond. Sometimes, we have to find a way and the strength to keep going. Right now, it may seem hopeless to keep trying to move on with your life. In this case, may this scripture, "The grace of our Lord Jesus Christ be with you all. Amen (Philippians 4:23)." May these powerful words empower you with God's grace to run your race.

Poems of Purpose

The strategy of being creative to deal with your pain is part of your healing. I thought that if I wrote a few poems about my Diamond, it would help me to get over losing her in a beautiful way. Therefore, I have chosen three types of poetry: the Acrostic, the Cinquain, and the Haiku to express my feeling about Diamond.

The Acrostic poem is easy to compose. You just have to find some words that describe your loved one, and go for it. I chose to use the letters of Diamond's name for this poem.

DIAMOND

D is for Dedicated and Dutiful

I is for Irresistible and Illustrious

A is for Amazing and Amusing

M is for Masterful Muse

O is for Ostentatious and Omni- competent

N is for Naughty and Nice

D is for Dogone Delectable

The Cinquain poem usually has a five line pattern. I thought it would be interesting to tackle this poem because Diamond and her circle of friends loved to come visit her. Whenever her pack came over, they were happy as they explored the house together. Sometimes they would be mischievous, but most times, they had fun playing with toys.

Diamond and Friends

Diamond

Contented, Charming

While roving through

The house with friends

Entertaining!

The Haiku is a Japanese poem with three lines with a pattern of five, seven, and five. I decided to compose this third poem about my Love for Diamond. She played a vital role in shaping my daily life by accepting me unconditionally. Once we had gotten to truly know and trust each other, it was clear that we had developed a special love with a strong bond like a mother and child shares.

Love for Diamond

Wide as the ocean,

Diamond,

My love for you

Eternally will last.

Healing Scriptures for Difficult Times

Dear Readers,

These scriptures should bring comfort to you when you feel the heaviness of the loss of your beloved. May you read and meditate on them as you try to adapt, adjust, and develop a new life without that special one who made you laugh, cry, and just encounter life, as you could not have not imagined. Experience and enjoy the calming scriptures of David, John, Matthew, Isaiah, and others.

Psalms 23:1-6 - The LORD is my shepherd; I shall not want.

Psalms 31:9-10 - Have mercy upon me, O LORD, for I am in trouble: mine eye is consumed with grief, yea, my soul and my belly.

Psalms 73:26 - My flesh and my heart faileth: but God is the strength of my heart, and my portion for ever.

Psalms 127:3 - Lo, children are an heritage of the LORD: and the fruit of the womb is his reward.

Psalms 34:18 - The LORD is nigh unto them that are of a broken heart; and saveth such as be of a contrite spirit.

Ecclesiastes 3:1-14 - To every thing there is a season, and a time to every purpose under the heaven:

2 A time to be born, and a time to die; a time to plant, and a time to pluck up that which is planted;

3 A time to kill, and a time to heal; a time to break down, and a time to build up;

4 A time to weep, and a time to laugh; a time to mourn, and a time to dance;

5 A time to cast away stones, and a time to gather stones together; a time to embrace, and a time to refrain from embracing;

6 A time to get, and a time to lose; a time to keep, and a time to cast away;

7 A time to rend, and a time to sew; a time to keep silence, and a time to speak;

[8] A time to love, and a time to hate; a time of war, and a time of peace.

[9] What profit hath he that worketh in that wherein he laboureth?

[10] I have seen the travail, which God hath given to the sons of men to be exercised in it.

[11] He hath made every thing beautiful in his time: also he hath set the world in their heart, so that no man can find out the work that God maketh from the beginning to the end.

[12] I know that there is no good in them, but for a man to rejoice, and to do good in his life.

[13] And also that every man should eat and drink, and enjoy the good of all his labour, it is the gift of God.

[14] I know that, whatsoever God doeth, it shall be for ever: nothing can be put to it, nor any thing taken from it: and God doeth it, that men should fear before him.

Malachi 4:2 But unto you that fear my name shall the Sun of righteousness arise with healing in his wings; and ye shall go forth, and grow up as calves of the stall.

1 Peter 5:7 - Casting all your care upon him; for he careth for you.

Isaiah 26:3 - Thou wilt keep him in perfect peace, whose mind is stayed on thee: because he trusteth in thee.

Isaiah 53:4-6 - Surely he hath borne our griefs, and carried our sorrows: yet we did esteem him stricken, smitten of God, and afflicted.

Matthew 4:23 - And Jesus went about all Galilee, teaching in their synagogues, and preaching the gospel of the kingdom, and healing all manner of sickness and all manner of disease among the people.

Matthew 9:35 - And Jesus went about all the cities and villages, teaching in their synagogues, and preaching the gospel of the kingdom, and healing every sickness and every disease among the people.

Matthew 5:1-10 - And seeing the multitudes, he went up into a mountain: and when he was set, his disciples came unto him:

[2] And he opened his mouth, and taught them, saying,

[3] Blessed are the poor in spirit: for theirs is the kingdom of heaven.

[4] Blessed are they that mourn: for they shall be comforted.

[5] Blessed are the meek: for they shall inherit the earth.

[6] Blessed are they which do hunger and thirst after righteousness: for they shall be filled.

[7] Blessed are the merciful: for they shall obtain mercy.

8 Blessed are the pure in heart: for they shall see God.

9 Blessed are the peacemakers: for they shall be called the children of God.

10 Blessed are they which are persecuted for righteousness' sake: for theirs is the kingdom of heaven.

Matthew 11:28-30 - Come unto me, all [ye] that labour and are heavy laden, and I will give you rest.

John 3:16 - For God so loved the world, that he gave his only begotten Son, that whosoever believeth in him should not perish, but have everlasting life.

Luke 9:6 -And they departed, and went through the towns, preaching the gospel, and healing every where.

Luke 9:11- And the people, when they knew it, followed him: and he received them, and spake unto them of the kingdom of God, and healed them that had need of healing.

1 Thessalonians 4:13 - But I would not have you to be ignorant, brethren, concerning them which are asleep, that ye sorrow not, even as others which have no hope.

John 11:35 - Jesus wept.

John 14:1 - Let not your heart be troubled: ye believe in God, believe also in me.

John 14:27 - Peace I leave with you, my peace I give unto you: not as the world giveth, give I unto you. Let not your heart be troubled, neither let it be afraid.

John 16:16 - A little while, and ye shall not see me: and again, a little while, and ye shall see me, because I go to the Father.

2 Corinthians 1:3-4 - Blessed be God, even the Father of our Lord Jesus Christ, the Father of mercies, and the God of all comfort;

1 Peter 5:7 - Casting all your care upon him; for he careth for you.

Revelation 21:4 - And God shall wipe away all tears from their eyes; and there shall be no more death, neither sorrow, nor crying, neither shall there be any more pain: for the former things are passed away.

Revelation 22:2- In the midst of the street of it, and on either side of the river, was there the tree of life, which bare twelve manner of fruits, and yielded her fruit every month: and the leaves of the tree were for the healing of the nations.

Free

When you look up to the sky, and take a picture of the sun, the rays shine so brilliantly. It is then that you know you are free. This is what the sun brings- freedom! Diamond, girl you are free!

From Sunrise, April 5, 2009 – To – Sunset, April 15, 2015

Thank you Diamond for your loving lasting foot prints. Diamond you will forever have a lasting imprint in my heart!

I love you much…always my Diva-Darling!

Diamond's Rainbow

God put the rainbow in the sky as a beautiful promise to Noah, his descendents, and all living creature of all flesh. This covenant provided that He would never flood the whole earth again destroying all flesh. In Genesis 9:16 (KJV), God said, "And the bow shall be in the cloud; and I will look upon it, that I may remember the everlasting covenant between God and every living creature of all flesh that is upon the earth."

Thank you for the beauty you brought to my life Diamond. In fact, a full radiant rainbow appeared in your room's doorway on Tuesday 16th of April 2015. As I was leaving your room, the rainbow was there. I remember looking at this amazing site in the doorway, and I had to go back into the doorway to see it again.

In my mind, I asked myself, how could a rainbow appear here without the sun? Again, I looked back at the window, but I did not see anything. Therefore, I reasoned that it probably came from the light through the blinds. Now, I know this was your amazing way of telling me and showing me that all is well, and that you made it over the rainbow!

May you rest in peace (RIP) Diamond. You know we loved you and that you will forever live in our hearts.

About The Author

Shelia Hampton, the author of, **Broken and Scattered into Pieces *but Made Whole Again, 2009*,** loves being an entrepreneur, poet, inspirational and motivational speaker, life coach, event planner, volunteer, and mentor. She is a loving wife, mother of two beautiful children, a gracious grandmother, and a fun-loving foster parent to many, and a deacon at her church. She has received an array of awards that demonstrate her worthiness of her achievements and growth. She is a proud founder of Christian Women Intertwining Network (WIN), a women's confidential support group with a mission to uplift, encourage, and empower women in all areas of their lives. Additionally, this network mentors and counsels while teaching excellence, positive thinking, self-esteem, healthy living, and sisterhood while raising social awareness in problem areas by enhancing social health through education and economic independence.

Mrs. Hampton is a true native of Washington DC who enjoys doing God's work to accomplish extraordinary endeavors that will bless lives. **Shelia** has an anointed direction from God to assist others with their life's struggles. As a Deacon of Ministry at The Ark of Safety Christian Church, she seeks to help others by empowering them through God's word to accept daily challenges as inevitable but winnable, through His wisdom. She is the Founder/CEO of Shelia Hampton Ministries and has been an educational advocate and mentor for over 30 years. Shelia was the Founder/CEO of Righteous Corner Learning Center (RCLC) 2003-2009. She was awarded an (MBE) Minority Business Enterprise Award in 2008 and was placed in the Top 100 Businesses in DC, MD, and VA.

Shelia has purposed this book to empower animal lovers, who have lost their pets to death, to find peace during their storm by sharing Diamond's Story. Her Motto is, "When God Speaks, I Listen. The word of God, in John 14:1-3 (KJV) says, "Let not your heart be troubled: ye believe in God, believe also in me." Therefore, when we lose someone or something, we can be comforted once we give the problem to Him. He will give us the wisdom to move on with our lives. Helping animal-lovers maneuver through the grief process to find tranquility after the loss of their beloved pets is the specific goal of my book. Mrs. Hampton asserts that, "through proper adaptations, adjustments, strategies, and steps, they can become "whole again" because with God--all things are possible to those who believe.

Contact Us

To request author to speak, the
contact information is as follows:

Email: hamp.shelia@gmail.com

Phone: 1(301)-848-5016

Address: Shelia Hampton

P.O. Box 917

Accokeek, MD 20607

About The Book

In this book, Shelia Hampton is taking you on a journey through an unanticipated heartache in her life. Diamond passed away in early April 2015 after suffering from an illness 2015. Her first book, **Broken And Scattered Into Pieces**, ***But Made Whole Again (2009)***, makes plain the fact that life is not always what you expect it to be, but with God's guidance, no matter what you are facing, you can make it through any struggle and pain that comes your way. Shelia has chosen to share how she acquired Diamond and to showcase the good times they have shared. It is her wish that all animal lovers will be blessed as they read about their good times together, look at their perky pictures, and process the poetic verses.

"**Diamond** was one of the great loves of my life. When I thought that I was rescuing her when she needed someone to care for her, she was actually liberating me with her unconditional love," recounts Mrs. Hampton. "We have all struggled with something or somebody. Diamond came into my life when I wasn't looking for a pet or someone to comfort me, but that is exactly what she did---comfort me. Now that she is gone, I can really see what a true blessing she had added to my life. Ms. Diamond set me free to be me! Her loving and caring ways salvaged some pain that I did not know I was enduring. I want to thank God for sending Diamond my way to bless me immeasurably.

Shelia will give you some strategies to help you get over the grief of someone or something that you have lost. These steps and sound solutions have been taken from her own experiences. She is hopeful that they will be beneficial to you in some significant, comforting way. Diamond is deeply missed by me, but I know that she is in a better place. Mark 11:22-24 (KJV), "And Jesus answering saith unto them, Have faith in God. For verily I say unto you, That whosoever shall say unto this mountain, Be thou removed, and be thou cast into the sea; and shall not doubt in his heart, but shall believe that those things which he saith shall come to pass; he shall have whatsoever he saith. Therefore I say unto you, What things soever ye desire, when ye pray, believe that ye receive them, and ye shall have them. God will give you guidance and peace through all of your troubled and trying times. You will make it through with His grace and mercy! "Diamond, rest in peace sweet girl!"

Love,

Mom

Shelia believes that Diamond went to "Doggie Heaven" after she died. Mrs. Hampton titled this book, "Diamond's Everlasting Foot Prints" to reveal the everlasting impressions that the imprints of Diamond's love made and have upon her heart.

Made in the USA
Middletown, DE
15 May 2019